Katie CAN do... and you CAN too!

Katie Hull

Glossary by Nancy K. Smith, R.N.

ISBN: 1490569774

ISBN 13: 9781490569772

Library of Congress Control Number: 2013912179

CreateSpace Independent Publishing Platform

North Charleston, South Carolina

Acknowledgements

There are so many people who have helped me to have a "can do" attitude and who have inspired me to try new things. I wish to thank my parents, Bryant and Sarah Hull, who believed in me from the very beginning and who help and encourage me to achieve my dreams. I am thankful to my grandmother Nancy Smith. She assisted me in writing this book, and her experience as a registered nurse has helped me as I recovered from many surgeries. Judy Reynolds, RN, or "Nurse Judy," as we call her, has assisted me since pre-school with many of my special needs at school. Her love and support has lifted me up during good and not-so-good days. Dr. Monica Rogerson, my adaptive physical education teacher involves me in adaptive sports and activities. Emi Yukawa, my physical therapist, helps with my mobility and adaptive goals. The amazing teachers and staff at my school have been so supportive and caring. Jennifer Kumiyama, Mary Zendejas, and Chelsie Hill, some of my friends who use wheelchairs, have been wonderful role models of people who have followed their dreams and have turned disabilities in to abilities. I want to give a big thank you to my wheelchair sport coach, Rick Tirambulo, who always encourages me to try new sports and to do my best.

I also wish to thank the following organizations that have assisted me in many of my adaptive activities: Life Rolls On; Camp Nugget at California State University, Long Beach; Rancho Los Amigos Rehabilitation; Adaptive Recreation Center in Big Bear, California; and Colours Wheelchair, whose chairs make all of my wheelchair activities possible.

Thank you to the doctors, nurses, and staff at Loma Linda Medical Center and Children's Hospital of Orange County for helping me through all of my treatments and surgeries. Your kind care is so appreciated by my family and me.

I am SO grateful to my sister and brother, Ella and Carter, and to my extended family and friends for their support and love.

Here I am with my sister and brother.

The doctor came in to the hospital room and told my parents that the problem was worse than he thought. He said that I would never be able to walk.

My name is Katie. My real name is Katherine, but everyone calls me Katie, and this is my story.

Ten years ago, when my mom was pregnant with me, the doctors found out that something was wrong. At the beginning, they didn't know exactly what the problem was. They told my mom and dad it was serious and that I might not live. Later, when they did more tests, the doctors told my parents that I would be born with **spina bifida**, which is when part of the **spinal cord** is not in the right place. This can cause problems with your feet, legs, and other things.

My parents hold the ultrasound picture of me.

The day I was born, my parents were so happy to see me, and they loved me right away! I had surgery soon after I was born to put my spinal cord in place.

Mom cuddles me the day after my first surgery.

My mom and dad took me home from the hospital a few days later. I was a happy baby and loved being held and snuggled.

My parents love watching me laugh and play.

As I grew, I slowly learned to crawl and finally began walking using a **walker** and wearing foot and ankle **braces**. I named my first walker "Bob." A health care professional, called a physical therapist, worked with me as I was learning these new things.

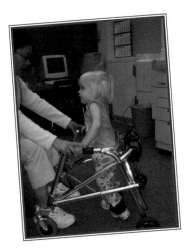

This is a foot and ankle brace.

It was hard to walk because my feet and parts of my legs are **paralyzed.**

My physical therapist helped me
learn to walk using my walker, "Bob."

I would fall down sometimes when I was learning to walk. That was not fun. I learned quickly that the important thing to do when something is difficult is to get back up and keep on trying!

My sister likes to help me.

Here I am on my first day of kindergarten.

Now I have to use my wheelchair more often, but sometimes I use **forearm crutches** to walk short distances.

Getting ready to go on a zip line.

With my crutches, braces, and back
pack on, I'm all ready for school.

Some kids stare at me because they think that I can't do very many things since I use **adaptive equipment**, but they should really try to get to know me before they decide what I can't do. I am able to do much more than they might think.

Some of my favorite things to do are skiing, surfing, wheelchair racing, swimming, tennis, and basketball. I like to learn new things and have fun with my friends and family.

Mom and I are ready to zoom down the hill.

Most people ski standing up, using their legs and feet. I can ski too, but I use my arms and upper body. I sit in a monoski, also known as a "sit ski," which is kind of like a sled with one ski down the middle. In order to turn, I use my upper body to lean in the direction I want to move, using my adaptive ski poles, called outriggers, to stay balanced.

Outriggers and some help from a ski volunteer keep me from falling over in the monoski.

As I swoosh down the soft, white snow, I feel like I'm floating on a cloud.

Here I go!

Whoosh!

Surfing is really fun! Many people stand up on a surfboard when they catch a wave in the ocean. When I surf, I lie on my tummy and my dad helps me ride the waves. I use my arms to paddle around in the water. I like how the powerful waves push me through the beautiful ocean.

My dad and I love to surf in the waves.

I got the chance to surf because of a group of volunteers who help kids like me to enjoy water sports. I have discovered that there are so many nice people in this world who like to bring happiness to others and I am thankful for them.

Swim goggles help to keep the salt water out of my eyes when I surf.

When I go to the beach, we often rent a beach wheelchair at one of the lifeguard stations. Most regular wheelchairs do not work very well on sand. A beach wheelchair, with its big wheels, can move smoothly on the sand.

Exploring the shoreline is fun in a beach wheelchair!

My dad helps me roll through the sand and the shallow water in the beach wheelchair. I like to explore the tide pools and look for shells on the sand. When my dad pushes me through the waves, it feels like I am riding on a roller coaster.

Rolling around in the shallow water makes me laugh.

Ready...set...go! I began wheelchair racing when I was just a little girl. I used my regular wheelchair when I first began racing.

My first race was exciting!

I did it!

When I got a little older, I started using a sports wheelchair to race. Because I use my arms so much, my upper body is strong, so when I race in my sports wheelchair I can go superfast and turn as quick as lightning.

Do you think I beat my dad in this race?

Wearing racing gloves protects my hands from getting blisters.

It took me quite a long time to learn to swim, since my legs and feet don't work very well. I decided to keep on trying no matter how hard it was, so I made an effort to kick my legs and use my arms to glide. I finally was able to swim, and now it's my favorite sport.

Learning to swim was hard work.

I'm trying to learn how to kick my legs.
Can you tell by my face that it took a lot of effort?

Now I enjoy swimming in pools and at the bay. I always make sure to swim with a buddy. When I float through the water, I feel like a beautiful mermaid who is as light as a feather.

Is this a mermaid or me?

Playing tennis and basketball is sometimes hard to do in a wheelchair. It takes practice and patience, but I always have fun, even if I get a little hurt or lose a game. When I play tennis, I use my wheelchair to spin around the court while I swing at the ball with my racquet.

The ball bounces off my racquet as fast as a rocket!

Basketball is fun too. I dribble the ball with one hand while I push my chair around the court with my other hand, changing hands with each push and dribbling until I pass the ball to another player or try to throw the ball into the basket. I'm not the best at making baskets, but I keep trying.

Let's play basketball!

Sometimes people feel sorry for me because I use a wheelchair to get places. I don't feel sad, though, because there are so many things that I CAN do! All people are different, with their own strengths and weaknesses. The key is to do your best at what you CAN do and learn to adapt to the things you can't do. It might be more difficult to do some things, but with a positive attitude and lots of work, disabilities can become abilities and we CAN do many things!

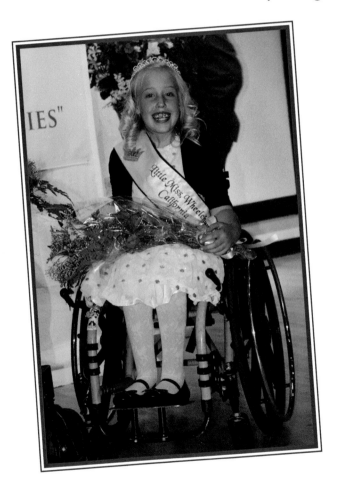

Here I am as Little Miss Wheelchair, California

You CAN do it!

Glossary

Adaptive equipment: These are tools that assist people with disabilities in activities of daily living. Some types of adaptive equipment include wheelchairs, walkers, crutches, standing frames, and bath chairs. Other adaptive equipment such as racing wheelchairs, monoskis, and tricycles can be used for recreational activities.

Braces: Orthotic braces help people who have weak feet and legs. The brace gives them support when they walk. They are usually made of plastic with Velcro straps and are custom made to fit correctly.

Forearm crutches: This type of crutch has a cuff at the top to go around the lower part of the arm (forearm). It is used by putting the arm into cuff and holding the grip. Crutches are used for people who cannot use their legs to support all of their weight.

Paralyzed (Paralysis): Paralysis is when certain muscles do not work, and it usually also means that the person cannot feel the part of the body that is paralyzed. Paralysis is often caused by damage to the nervous system, especially in the spinal cord.

Spina bifida: When a baby is growing inside of the mother, sometimes part of the bones on the back (vertebrae) do not form correctly, causing the spinal cord to come through an opening between the bones. Spina bifida can be closed at birth with surgery, but this does not bring back normal function to the part of the spinal cord that was damaged.

Spinal cord: The spinal cord is a long, thin bundle of nerve tissue that extends from the brain down to the middle part of the back. The spinal cord is part of the central nervous system, which sends messages to and from the brain and other parts of the body.

Walker: A walker is a tool for people who need support while walking. It is about waist high. Many walkers have two front and two back wheels. With the frame surrounding their front and sides, people using the walker hold on to the sides of the frame with both hands and push the walker to move forward.